PONTIFICAL COUNCIL FOR THE FAMILY

PREPARATION
FOR THE SACRAMENT
OF MARRIAGE

FAMILY PUBLICATIONS

CATHOLIC TRUTH SOCIETY
PUBLISHERS TO THE HOLY SEE

PONTIFICAL COUNCIL FOR THE FAMILY

PREPARATION
FOR THE SACRAMENT
OF MARRIAGE

© LIBRERIA EDITRICE VATICANA

published by
FAMILY PUBLICATIONS
77 BANBURY ROAD · OXFORD OX2 6LF
Tel: **01865 514408**   *Fax:* **01865 552774**
ISBN 1 871217 20 2

CATHOLIC TRUTH SOCIETY
192 VAUXHALL BRIDGE ROAD · LONDON SW1V 1PD
Tel: **0171 834 4392**   *Fax:* **0171 630 1124**
ISBN 1 86082 002 6

printed in England by
BPC Wheatons Ltd, Exeter

CONTENTS

CONTENTS

INTRODUCTION

1.   Preparation for marriage, for married and family life, is of great importance for the good of the Church. In fact, the sacrament of Marriage has great value for the whole Christian community and, in the first place, for the spouses whose decision is such that it cannot be improvised or made hastily. In the past, this preparation could count on the support of society which recognized the values and benefits of marriage. Without any difficulties or doubts, the Church protected the sanctity of marriage with the awareness that this sacrament represented an ecclesial guarantee as the living cell of the People of God. At least in the communities that were truly evangelized, the Church's support was solid, unitary and compact. In general, separations and marriage failures were rare, and divorce was considered a social "plague" (cf. *Gaudium et Spes = GS,* 47).

Today, on the contrary, in many cases, we are witnessing an accentuated deterioration of the family and a certain corrosion of the values of marriage. In many nations, especially economically developed ones, the number of marriages has decreased. Marriage is usually contracted at a later age and the number of divorces and separations is increasing, even during the first years of married life. All this inevitably leads to a pastoral concern that comes up repeatedly: Are the persons contracting marriage really prepared for it? The problem of preparation for the sacrament of Marriage and the life that follows emerges as a great pastoral need, first for the sake of the spouses, for

1

the whole Christian community and for society. Therefore, interest in, and initiatives for providing adequate and timely answers to preparation for the sacrament of Marriage are growing everywhere.

2. Through ongoing contact with the Episcopal Conferences and the Bishops in various meetings, and especially their *ad limina* visits, the Pontifical Council for the Family has carefully followed the pastoral concern regarding the preparation and celebration of the sacrament of Marriage and the life that follows. The Council has been repeatedly asked to offer an instrument for the preparation of Christian engaged persons which the present document represents. The Council has also drawn on the contributions from many Apostolic Movements, Groups and Associations working for the pastoral care of the family who have offered their support, advice and experience for the preparation of these guidelines.

Marriage preparation constitutes a *providential and favourable* period for those oriented toward this Christian sacrament, and a *Kayrós,* i.e., a period in which God calls upon the engaged and helps them discern the vocation to marriage and family life. The engagement period is set within the context of a rich evangelization process. In fact, questions that affect the family converge in the life of the engaged, the future spouses. They are therefore invited to understand the meaning of the responsible and mature love of the community of life and love which their family will be, a real domestic church which will contribute toward enriching the whole Church.

The importance of this preparation involves a process of evangelization which is both maturation and deepening in the faith. If the faith is weak or almost non-existent (cf.

2

Familiaris Consortio = FC 68), it must be revived. Thorough, patient instruction that arouses and nourishes the ardour of a living faith cannot be excluded. Especially where the environment has become *paganized*, it will be particularly advisable to offer a "journey of faith, which is similar to the catechumenate" *(FC* 66), and a presentation of the fundamental Christian truths that may help acquire or strengthen the maturity of the faith of the persons contracting marriage. It would be desirable if the favourable moment of marriage preparation could he transformed, as a sign of hope, into a New Evangelization for the future families.

3.   This particular attention is highlighted by the teachings of the Second Vatican Council *(GS* 52), the guidelines of the Papal Magisterium *(FC* 66), the ecclesial norms themselves *(Codex Iuris Canonici = CIC,* can. 1063; *Codex Canonum Ecclesiarum Orientalium = CCEO,* can. 783), the *Catechism of the Catholic Church* (n. 1632), and other documents of the Magisterium, including the *Charter of the Rights of the Family.* The two most recent documents of the Papal Magisterium – the Letter to Families *Gratissimam Sane* and the Encyclical *Evangelium Vitae (= EV)* – constitute a notable aid for our task.

In response to repeated requests, as we have said, the Pontifical Council for the Family *began* reflection on the subject by concentrating more on "preparation courses", in line with the Apostolic Exhortation *Familiaris Consortio.* During its preparation, the present document *went through* the following editorial process.

In 1991, the Council dedicated its General Assembly (September 30 - October 5) to the theme of preparation for the sacrament of Marriage. The Presidential Committee of the Pontifical Council for the Family and the married couples

3

who are part of the Council offered ample material for a first draft. Later, from July 8-13, 1992, a working group was convened made up of pastors, consultors and experts who prepared a second draft which was sent to the Episcopal Conferences for their contributions and additional suggestions. A great number of responses with useful suggestions came in, and these were studied and included in a subsequent draft prepared by a working group in 1995. This Council now presents the guideline document which is offered as a basis for the pastoral work related to preparation for the sacrament of Marriage. It will be especially useful for the Episcopal Conferences in the preparation of their Directories, and also for a greater pastoral commitment in dioceses, parishes and apostolic movements (cf. *FC* 66).

4. The "Magna Carta" for families, the Apostolic Exhortation *Familiaris Consortio,* which has already been cited, had already pointed out that: " . . . the changes that have taken place within almost all modern societies demand that not only the family but also society and the Church should be involved in the effort of properly preparing young people for their future responsibilities. (...) The Church must therefore promote better and more intensive programmes of marriage preparation, in order to eliminate as far as possible the difficulties that many married couples find themselves in, and even more in order to favour positively the establishing and maturing of successful marriages" (*FC* 66).

The Code of Canon Law states that there should be "personal preparation for entering marriage, so that the spouses are disposed to the holiness and the obligations of their new state" (*CIC* can. 1063, 2, *CCEO* can. 783, §1). These instructions are also found in the *Ordo celebrandi matrimonium* 12.

In his Address to the Ninth General Assembly of the Pontifical Council for the Family (October 4, 1991), the Holy Father added: "The greater the difficulties caused by one's surroundings for knowing the truth of the Christian sacrament and of the institution of marriage, all the greater must be our efforts to prepare spouses adequately for their responsibilities". Then, with some more concrete observations regarding the courses as such, he went on to say: "You have been able to observe that, given the necessity of having such courses in parishes, in consideration of the positive results of the various methods used, it seems appropriate to start drawing up criteria to be adopted, in the form of a guide or directory, to offer the particular Churches a valuable aid". This is all the more so because in the particular Churches, for much of "the 'people of life and the people for life', *the family has a decisive responsibility*. This responsibility flows from its very nature as a community of life and love, founded upon marriage, and from its mission to 'guard, reveal and communicate love'" (*EV* 92 and cf. *FC* 17).

5. For this purpose, the Pontifical Council for the Family offers this document which has as its object the preparation for the sacrament of Marriage and its celebration.

The guidelines that emerge constitute an itinerary for the *remote, proximate and immediate preparation for the sacrament of Marriage* (cf. *FC* 66). The material provided herein is addressed first of all to the Episcopal Conferences, the individual Bishops and their co-workers in the pastoral care of marriage preparation, and it is also addressed to the engaged themselves who are the object of the Church's pastoral concern.

6.   Particular pastoral attention will be given to the engaged in special situations foreseen by the *CIC* can. 1071, 1072 and 1125, and by the *CCEO* can. 789 and 814. When the guidelines presented in the document cannot be applied completely in their regard, they can still be useful in guiding and accompanying them in a fitting way.

Faithful to the will and teaching of Christ, through her own legislation the Church expresses her pastoral charity in her care for all the situations of the faithful. The criteria offered are means for providing help in a positive way and should not be understood as further, constrictive requirements.

7.   The underlying doctrinal motivation that inspires this document comes from the conviction that marriage is a value that takes its origin from the Creation and that it is rooted in human nature. "Have you not read that he who made them from the beginning made them male and female, and said, 'For this reason a man shall leave his father and mother and be joined to his wife, and the two shall become one?'" (*Matthew* 19: 4-5). Therefore, what the Church does for the family and marriage certainly contributes to the good of society as such and to the good of all. Furthermore, as an expression of the new life made possible by the Risen Christ, Christian marriage always expresses the truth about married love and is like a prophecy that clearly proclaims a human being's real needs: that man and woman are called upon from the beginning to live in a communion of life and love and that this complementarity will lead to strengthening the human dignity of the spouses, the good of the children and of society itself, through " . . . *the defence and promotion of life . . . everyone's task and responsibility*" (*EV* 91).

8. Therefore, the present document takes into consideration both the natural human realities proper to this divine institution, and the specific ones of the sacrament instituted by Christ. It is divided into three parts:

1) The Importance of Preparation for Christian Marriage;
2) The Stages or Periods of Preparation;
3) The Celebration of Marriage.

I

THE IMPORTANCE OF PREPARATION FOR CHRISTIAN MARRIAGE

9. The starting-point for an itinerary of marriage preparation is the awareness that the marriage covenant was taken up and raised to a sacrament of the New Covenant by the Lord Jesus Christ, through the power of the Holy Spirit. The sacrament joins the spouses to the self-giving love of Christ the Bridegroom for the Church, his Bride (cf. *Ephesians* 5: 25-32) by making them the image of, and sharers in this love. It makes them give praise to the Lord, it sanctifies the conjugal union and the life of the Christian faithful who celebrate it, and gives rise to the Christian family, the domestic church, the "first and living cell of society" (*Apostolicam Actuositatem*, 11), and the *"sanctuary of life"* (*EV* 92 and also 6, 88, 94). Therefore, the sacrament is celebrated and lived in the heart of the New Covenant, i.e. the paschal mystery. It is Christ, the Bridegroom in our midst (cf. *Gratissimam Sane,* 18; *Matthew* 9: 15), who is the source of its energies. Therefore, Christian couples and families are neither isolated nor alone.

For Christians, marriage, which has its origin in God the Creator, also implies a real vocation to a particular state and a life of grace. In order to be brought to its maturation, this vocation requires adequate, particular preparation and a specific path of faith and love, all the more so because this vocation is given to a couple for the good of the Church and society. This has all the meaning and strength of a public commitment made before God and society that goes beyond individual limits.

10. As a community of life and love, both as a natural divine institution and a sacrament, marriage always possesses a source of formidable energies (cf. *FC* 43), no matter what difficulties there may be. Through the witness of the spouses, marriage can become Good News, contributing greatly to the new evangelization, and ensuring the future of society. However, these energies must be discovered, appreciated and enhanced by the spouses themselves and by the ecclesial community in the period preceding the celebration of marriage that constitutes its preparation.

Many dioceses around the world are making efforts to find forms for an increasingly effective marriage preparation. Many positive experiences have been passed on to the Pontifical Council for the Family. No doubt these experiences will be consolidated more and more and provide valid assistance if they are known and appreciated within the Episcopal Conferences and by *each Bishop* in the pastoral care of the local Churches.

What is called *Preparation* in this document includes a broad and thorough process of *education* for married life which must be considered in the totality of its values. This is why if the current psychological and cultural situation is taken into consideration, marriage preparation represents an urgent need. In fact, preparation is educating for the respect and care for life which, in the Sanctuary of families, must become a real and proper culture of human life in all its manifestations and stages for those who are part of the people *of* life and *for* life (cf. *EV* 6, 78, 105). The very reality of marriage is so rich that it first requires a process of sensitization so that the engaged will feel the need to prepare themselves for it. Therefore, pastoral care of the family should direct its best efforts towards qualifying that preparation, also making use of pedagogical and psychological aids that have a sound orientation.

In another document published recently (December 8, 1995) by the Pontifical Council for the Family entitled, *The Truth and Meaning of Human Sexuality: Guidelines for Education Within the Family*, the Council tries to help families in their task of educating their children with regard to sexuality.

11. Lastly, because of the present circumstances which were mentioned earlier, the Church's concern has become more urgent with regard to marriage preparation. On the one hand, the recovery of values and some important aspects of marriage and the family can be observed together with the flourishing of joyful testimonies by countless Christian spouses and families. However, on the other hand, the number of persons is increasing who ignore or reject the riches of marriage with a form of mistrust that goes so far as to doubt or reject its goods and values (cf. *GS* 48). Today we see with alarm the spread of a "culture" or a mentality that has lost heart with regard to the family as a necessary value for spouses, children and society. Some attitudes and some measures envisaged in laws do not help the family based on marriage and even deny its rights. As a matter of fact, a secularized atmosphere has been spreading in different parts of the world which *especially* affects young people and subjects them to the pressure of a secularized environment in which one ends up losing the meaning of God and consequently the deep meaning of spousal love and the family as well. Is it not denying the truth of God to shut out

the very origin and source of this intimate mystery? (cf. *GS* 22). The negation of God in its different forms often includes the rejection of the institutions and structures which are part of God's plan, and which have been laid down since Creation (cf. *Matthew* 19: 3ss). As a result, everything is interpreted as being the fruit of human will and/or consensus that can change.

12. In countries where the process of de-Christianization is more prevalent, the disturbing crisis of moral values stands out, in particular, the loss of the identity of marriage and the Christian family and hence the meaning of engagement. In addition to these losses, there is a crisis of values within the family itself to which a climate of widespread and even legalized permissiveness contributes. This is greatly encouraged by the communications media that present contrary models as if they were real values. What seems to be a cultural fabric is formed, offered to the new generations as an alternative to the concept of conjugal life and marriage, its sacramental value, and its links with the Church.

Phenomena which confirm these situations and reinforce such a culture are connected with new lifestyles which devalue the human dimensions of the contracting parties with disastrous consequences for the family. These include sexual permissiveness, the decrease in marriages or their continuous postponement, the increase in divorces, the contraceptive mentality, the spread of deliberate abortion, the spiritual void and deep dissatisfaction which contribute to the spread of drugs, alcoholism, violence and suicide among young people and adolescents.

In other areas of the world, situations of under-development including extreme poverty and misery, as well as the simultaneous presence of cultural elements against or outside the Christian vision make both the stability of the family and building up an in-depth education in Christian love difficult and precarious.

13. Permissive laws contribute toward aggravating the situation with all their force in forging a mentality that harms families (cf. *EV* 59) with regard to divorce, abortion and sexual freedom. Many means of communication[1] spread and help strengthen a climate of permissiveness and form what seems to be a cultural fabric that impedes young people from their normal growth in the Christian faith, their ties with the Church, and their discovery of the sacramental value of marriage and the requirements derived from its celebration. It is true that education for marriage has always been necessary, but a Christian culture made its formulation and assimilation easier. Today this is sometimes more arduous and more urgent.

14. For all these reasons, in the Apostolic Exhortation *Familiaris Consortio* – which brings together the results of the 1980 Synod on the Family – His Holiness John Paul II indicates that "More than ever necessary in our times is preparation of young people for marriage and family life" (*FC* 66). He urges the promotion of "better and more intensive programmes of marriage preparation, in order to eliminate as far as possible the difficulties that many married couples find themselves in, and even more in order to favour positively the establishing and maturing of successful marriages" (*Ibid.*).

---

[1] This theme was reflected on during the international meeting organized from June 2-4, 1993 by the Pontifical Council for the Family in collaboration with the Pontifical Council for Social Communications.

Along the same lines, and in order to respond in an organic way to the current threats and demands, it seems timely for the Episcopal Conferences to publish with some urgency "a *Directory for the Pastoral Care of the Family*" (*Ibid.*). In such Directories, the elements considered necessary for a more incisive pastoral care should be sought and delineated which aim at recovering the Christian identity of marriage and the family so that the family itself will succeed in being a community of persons at the service of human life and the faith, the first and living cell of society, a believing and evangelizing community, a real "domestic church, centre of communion and ecclesial service" (*Ibid.*), "summoned to proclaim, celebrate and serve the *Gospel of life*" (*EV* 92, and also 28, 78, 79, 105).

15. Given the importance of the theme, and aware of the different initiatives which have been made in this direction by not a few Episcopal Conferences and many diocesan Bishops, the Pontifical Council for the Family extends the invitation to continue in this pastoral service with renewed commitment. The Episcopal Conferences have prepared useful material that can contribute to marriage preparation and following up family life. In continuity with the directives of the Apostolic See, the Pontifical Council offers these starting points for reflection *with exclusive reference to one part of the above-mentioned Directory*: that related to preparation for the sacrament of Marriage. Hence this part of the directory can be more useful in delineating and developing those aspects which are necessary for the proper preparation for marriage and Christian family life.

16. Alive in the tradition of the Church and deepened by the Magisterium, the Word of God stresses that marriage for

Christian spouses implies a response to God's vocation and the acceptance of the mission to be a sign of God's love for all the members of the human family, by partaking in the definitive covenant of Christ with the Church. Therefore, spouses become co-operators with the Creator and Saviour in the gift of love and life. Hence Christian marriage preparation can be described as a journey of faith which does not end with the celebration of marriage but continues throughout family life. Therefore, our perspective does not close with marriage as an act, at the moment of its celebration, but is ongoing. This is why preparation is also a "special opportunity for the engaged to rediscover and deepen the faith received in Baptism and nourished by their Christian upbringing. In this way they come to recognize and freely accept their vocation to follow Christ and to serve the Kingdom of God in the married state" (*FC* 51).

The Bishops are aware of the urgent and indispensable need to propose and articulate specific formation programmes in developing a process of Christian formation that is gradual and continuous (cf. *Ordo celebrandi matrimonium,* 15). In fact, it will useful to recall that real preparation is directed toward a conscious and free celebration of the sacrament of Marriage. However, this celebration is the source and expression of more binding and permanent implications.

17. From the experience of many pastors and educators it appears that the engagement period can be a time of mutual discovery but also of a deepening of faith. Therefore, it is a period of special supernatural gifts for personal and interpersonal spirituality. Unfortunately, for many, this period which is intended for human and Christian maturation, can be disturbed by an irresponsible use of sexuality which does not help spousal love to mature and, therefore, some

make a kind of apologia for premarital relations.

The successful outcome of the engaged couple's deepening in the faith is also conditioned by their previous formation. On the other hand, the way in which this period is lived will certainly have an influence on their future life as spouses and as a family. From this comes the decisive importance of the help offered to the engaged by their respective families and the whole ecclesial community. This also consists in prayer. In this regard, the blessing of the engaged which is foreseen in the *De benedictionibus* (nos. 195-214) is significant, in which the signs of this initial commitment are mentioned: the ring, the exchange of gifts and other customs (nos. 209-210). In any case, the human depth of the engagement should be recognized and saved from any commonplace approach.

Therefore, both the *riches* of marriage and the sacrament of Marriage, and the *decisive* importance of the engagement period – which today is often extended for years (with the various kinds of difficulties that this implies) – are reasons which call for the particular solidity of this formation.

18. It follows that the diocesan and parochial programming – with pastoral plans that give priority to the pastoral care of the family which enriches the whole of ecclesial life – presupposes that the formative task will find its proper place and development and that, between the dioceses and in the framework of the Episcopal Conferences, the best experiences can be evaluated and passed on in an exchange of pastoral experiences. It also seems important to know what forms of catechesis and education are given to adolescents regarding the various types of vocation and Christian love, what programmes are prepared for the engaged, the ways in which married couples are more mature

in the faith are included in this formation, as well as the best experiences aimed at creating a spiritual and cultural environment that is suitable for young people heading for marriage.

19. In the formation process, according to what is also referred to in the Apostolic Exhortation *Familiaris Consortio,* three stages or principal periods must be distinguished in marriage preparation: remote, proximate and immediate.

The particular goals of each stage will be achieved if – in addition to the fundamental human qualities and the basic truths of the faith – the engaged will also learn about the principal theological and liturgical content that marks the different phases of preparation. As a result, in the effort to adapt their life to those values, the engaged will acquire the true formation that prepares them for married life.

20. Marriage preparation must be set within the urgent need to evangelize culture – by permeating it to its *roots* (cf. Apostolic Exhortation *Evangelii Nuntiandi,* 19) – in everything that concerns the institution of marriage: making the Christian spirit penetrate minds and behaviour, as well as the laws and structures of the community where Christians live (cf. *Catechism of the Catholic Church,* n. 2105). This preparation, both implicitly and explicitly, constitutes one aspect of evangelization, so much so that it can deepen the strength of the Holy Father's affirmation: "The family is the heart of the New Evangelization" (...). The preparation itself "is a responsibility which first concerns married couples, called to be givers of life, on the basis of an ever greater *awareness of the meaning of procreation* as a unique event which clearly reveals that *human life is a gift received in order then to be given as a gift*" (*EV* 92).

In addition to religious values, abundant good and values that strengthen solidarity, respect, justice and forgiveness in personal and collective relations flow from marriage as the foundation of the family. In turn, the family, based on marriage, expects from society "*a recognition of its identity and an acceptance of its status as a subject in society*" (*Gratissimam Sane,* 17), and therefore to become "*the heart of the civilization of love*" (*Ibid.,* 13).

The whole diocese should be involved in this task and offer the proper support. The ideal would be to create a diocesan Commission for marriage preparation, including a group for the pastoral care of the family, composed of married couples with parish experience, movements and experts.

The task of this diocesan Commission would be formation, follow-up and co-ordination, in collaboration with centres on various levels involved in this service. The Commission should in turn be formed by networks of teams of chosen lay persons who work together in marriage preparation in a broad sense and not only in the courses. It should have the help of a co-ordinator, normally a priest, representing the bishop. If the co-ordination is entrusted to a lay person or a couple, a priest's assistance would be advisable.

All of this should enter into the organizational context of the diocese with its corresponding structures, such as possible areas headed by an Episcopal Vicar and vicars forane.

II

THE STAGES OR PERIODS
OF PREPARATION

21. The stages or periods which will be discussed are not rigidly defined. In fact, they cannot be defined either in relation to the age of the participants, nor in relation to their duration. However, it is useful to be familiar with them as working itineraries and instruments, especially for the content to be transmitted. They are broken up into remote, proximate and immediate preparation.

A. *Remote preparation*

22. Remote preparation includes infancy, childhood and adolescence and takes place first of all in the family and also in the school and formation groups, as a valid assistance to the family. This is the period in which respect for all authentic human values both in interpersonal and social relations is transmitted and instilled, with all this implies for the formation of character, self-control and self-esteem, the proper use of one's inclinations, and respect for persons of the other sex. Moreover, especially for Christians, a solid spiritual and catechetical formation is also required (cf. *FC* 66).

23. In the Letter to Families *Gratissimam Sane,* John Paul II mentions two fundamental truths in the task of education: "first, that man is called to live in truth and love; and

second, that everyone finds fulfilment through the sincere gift of self" (n. 16). Children's education thus begins before birth in the atmosphere in which the new life is awaited and welcomed, especially through the mother's loving dialogue with her child (cf. *Ibid.,* 16). This continues in childhood since education is "before all else *a reciprocal 'offering' on the part of both parents:* together they communicate their own mature humanity to the newborn child" (*Ibid.*). "In giving origin to a new life, parents recognize that the child, 'as the fruit of their mutual gift of love, is, in turn, a gift for both of them, a gift which flows from them'" (*EV* 92).

In its integral sense, which implies the transmission and basic growth of human and Christian values, Christian education – as the Second Vatican Council affirms – "not only develops the maturity of the human person . . ., but is especially directed towards ensuring that those who have been baptized, as they are gradually introduced to a knowledge of the mystery of salvation, become daily more appreciative of the gift of faith which they have received ... They should be trained to live their own lives in the new self, justified and sanctified through the truth" (*Gravissimum Educationis,* 2).

24. In this period, a faithful and courageous education in chastity and love as self-giving must not be lacking. Chastity is not a mortification of love but rather a condition for real love. In fact, if the vocation to married love is a vocation to self-giving in marriage, one must succeed in possessing oneself in order to be able to truly give oneself.

In this regard the sexual education received from parents in the first years of childhood and adolescence is important, as has been indicated in the document of this Pontifical Council for the Family mentioned earlier in n. 10.

25. In this stage of remote preparation some specific objectives should be achieved. Without pretending to make a complete list of them, as an indication it is noted that above all this preparation should attain the goal whereby every member of the faithful called to marriage will understand completely that, in the light of God's love, human love takes on a central role in Christian ethics. In fact, as a vocation and mission, human life is called to the love that has its source and end in God, "without excluding the possibility of the total gift of self to God in the vocation to the priestly or religious life" (*FC* 66). In this sense, it should be recalled that even when remote preparation deals more with doctrinal content of an anthropological nature, it is to be placed in the perspective of marriage in which human love becomes a sharing, as well as a sign, of the love between Christ and the Church. Therefore, married love makes present among mankind the same divine love made visible in the redemption. The journey or conversion from a rather external and vague level of faith, typical of many young people, to a discovery of the "Christian mystery" is both essential and decisive: a faith that involves the communion of Grace and love with the Risen Christ.

26. Remote preparation will have achieved its main goals if it succeeds in instilling the essentials for acquiring more and more the parameters of a right judgment regarding the hierarchy of values needed in choosing the best that society has to offer, according to St Paul's advice: " . . . test everything; hold fast what is good" (*1 Thessalonians* 5: 19). It should not be forgotten that, through the grace of God, love is also cherished, strengthened and intensified through the necessary values connected with giving, sacrifice, renunciation and self-denial. In this stage of formation,

pastoral help should already be directed toward making moral behaviour supported by faith. The example of parents, which becomes a real *witness* for those who will marry in the future, provides stimulus, support and consistency to this kind of *Christian lifestyle*.

27. 'This preparation will not lose sight of the importance of helping young people acquire a critical ability with regard to their surroundings, and the Christian courage of those who know how to be in the world without belonging to it. This is what we read in the *Letter to Diognetus*, a venerable and certainly authentic document from the early Christian era: "Christians are not distinguished from the rest of mankind by either country, speech, or customs . . . the whole tenor of their way of living stamps it as worthy of admiration and admittedly extraordinary . . . They marry like all others and beget children; but they do not expose their offspring. Their table they spread for all, but not their bed. They find themselves *in the flesh*, but do not live *according to the flesh*" (V, 1, 4, 6, 7, 8). Formation should arrive at a mentality and personality capable of not being led astray by ideas contrary to the unity and stability of marriage, thus able to react against the structures of the so-called *social sin* that "With greater or lesser violence, with greater or lesser harm, every sin has repercussions on the entire ecclesial body and the whole human family" (Apostolic Exhortation *Reconciliatio et Paenitentia,* 16). In the face of these sinful influences and so many social pressures, a critical conscience must be instilled.

28. A *Christian lifestyle*, witnessed to by Christian families, is in itself a form of evangelization and the very foundation of remote preparation. In fact, another goal of this stage is

the presentation of the parents' educational mission. It is in the family, the domestic church, that Christian parents are the first witnesses and educators of the children both in the growth of "faith, hope and charity", and in each child discovering his or her own vocation. *"Parents* are *the first and most important educators* of their own children, and they also possess a *fundamental competence* in this area: they are *educators because they are parents"* (*GS* 16). For this purpose parents need suitable and adequate assistance.

29. Among the types of assistance, the parish can be listed as the first place of Christian ecclesial formation. It is there that a style of living together as a *community* is learned (cf. *Sacrosanctum Concilium,* 42). Moreover, the school, other educational institutions, movements, groups, Catholic associations and, of course, associations of Christian families must not be overlooked.

Of particular importance in the educational processes of young people are the means of mass communication which ought to aid the family's mission in society in a positive way and not make it difficult.

30. This educational process must also be taken to heart by catechists, animators of the pastoral care of youth and vocations and, above all, pastors who will take advantage of homilies during liturgical celebrations and other forms of evangelization, personal meetings, and ways of Christian commitment, in order to stress and highlight the points that contribute to a preparation directed toward possible marriage (cf. *Ordo Celebrandi Matrimonium,* 14).

31. Therefore, the ways and means must be "invented" for the on-going formation of adolescents in the period preceding engagement which follows the stages of Christian initiation.

Exchanging information about the most appropriate experiences in this regard is extremely useful. Families joined together in the parishes, institutions and different forms of association, help create a social atmosphere in which responsible love will be healthy. Wherever it may be corrupted, for example, by pornography, they can react through the family's right. All of this is part of a "human ecology" (cf. *Centesimus Annus,* 38).

B. *Proximate preparation*

32. Proximate preparation takes place during the period of engagement. It consists of specific courses and must be distinguished from immediate preparation which is usually concentrated during the last meetings between engaged and pastoral workers before the celebration of the sacrament. During proximate preparation, it seems useful to provide the possibility to verify the maturation of the human values pertaining to the relationship of friendship and dialogue that should characterize the engagement. In view of the new state in life as a couple, the opportunity should be offered to deepen the life of faith, especially regarding knowledge about the sacramentality of the Church. This is an important stage of evangelization in which the faith must involve the personal and community dimensions both of the individual engaged persons and their families. In this process, it will also be possible to identify any difficulties they may have in living an authentic Christian life.

33. The period of proximate preparation generally coincides with the period of youth. Therefore it includes everything that pertains to the pastoral care of youth as such which is concerned with the integral growth of the faithful. The

pastoral care of youth cannot be separated from the framework of the family as if young people make up a kind of separate and independent "social class". It should reinforce the young people's social sense, first with regard to the members of their own family, and orient their values toward the future family they will have. The young people should have already been helped to discern their vocation through their own personal efforts and with the aid of the community, and above all the pastors. This discernment must take place before any commitment is made to get engaged. When the vocation to marriage is clear, it will be sustained first by grace and then by adequate preparation. The pastoral care of youth should also keep in mind that, because of various kinds of difficulties – such as a "prolonged adolescence" and remaining longer in one's family (a relatively new and troubling phenomenon), young people today tend to put off the commitment to get married for too long.

34. Proximate preparation should be based first of all on a catechesis sustained by listening to the Word of God, interpreted with the guidance of the Magisterium of the Church, in view of an ever greater understanding of the faith and giving witness to it in concrete life. Instruction should be offered in the context of a community of faith between families, especially in the parish, who participate and work in the formation of young people, according to their charisms and roles, and expand their influence to other social groups.

35. The engaged should receive instruction regarding the natural requirements of the interpersonal relationship between a man and a woman in God's plan for marriage and the

family: awareness regarding freedom of consent as the foundation of their union, the unity and indissolubility of marriage, the correct concept of responsible parenthood, the human aspects of conjugal sexuality, the conjugal act with its requirements and ends, and the proper education of children. All of this is aimed at knowing the moral truth and forming the personal conscience.

Proximate preparation should certainly ascertain whether the engaged have the basic elements of a psychological, pedagogical, legal and medical nature for marriage and family life. However, especially with regard to total self-giving and responsible procreation, the theological and moral formation will have to be given in a particular way. In fact, conjugal love is total, exclusive, faithful and fruitful (cf. *Humanae Vitae,* 9).

Today the scientific basis[2] of the natural methods for the regulation of fertility are recognized. Knowledge about these methods is useful. When there is just cause, their use must not only be a mere behavioural technique but be inserted into the pedagogy and process of the growth of love (cf. *EV* 97).

---

[2] These natural methods represent a valid alternative when couples have serious difficulties, for example of a health or economic nature, and they should also be offered in responsible and respectful demographic policies. The Pontifical Council for the Family held an international meeting with the promoters of the natural methods from December 9-11, 1992. The reports and contributions of the experts have been published in a text entitled: *Metodi Naturali per la regolazione della fertilità: l'alternativa autentica / The Natural Methods for the Regulation of Fertility: The Authentic Alternative.* The human sciences help theological reflection to grasp and deepen "*the difference, both anthropological and moral,* between contraception and recourse to the rhythm of the cycle" (*FC* 32).

Then the virtue of chastity will lead the spouses to practise periodic continence (cf. *Catechism of the Catholic Church,* nos. 2366-2371).

This preparation should also ensure that Christian engaged persons have correct ideas and a sincere "sentire cum ecclesia" regarding marriage itself, the mutual roles of a woman and a man in a couple, the family and society, sexuality and openness towards others.

36. Young people should also be helped to become aware of any psychological and/or emotional shortcomings they may have, especially the inability to open up to others, and any forms of selfishness that can take away from the total commitment of their self-giving. This help will also aid in discovering the potential and the need for human and Christian growth in their life. For this purpose, the persons in charge of marriage preparation should also be concerned with giving solid formation to the moral conscience of the engaged so that they will be prepared for the free and definitive choice of marriage which is expressed in the mutually exchanged consent before the Church in the marriage covenant.

37. During this stage of preparation, frequent meetings will be necessary in an atmosphere of dialogue, friendship and prayer, with the participation of pastors and catechists. They should stress the fact that "The family *celebrates the Gospel of life* through *daily prayer*, both individual prayer and family prayer. The family prays in order to glorify and give thanks to God for the gift of life, and implores his light and strength in order to face times of difficulty and suffering without losing hope" (*EV* 93). Moreover, Christian married couples who are apostolically committed, in a vision of sound

Christian optimism, can contribute to shedding greater light on Christian life in the context of the vocation to marriage and in the complementarity of all the vocations. Therefore, this period should not only be for theoretical study but also for formation during which the engaged, with the help of grace and by avoiding all forms of sin, will prepare to give themselves as a couple to Christ who sustains, purifies and ennobles the engagement and married life. In this way, premarital chastity takes on its full meaning and rules out any cohabitation, premarital relations, and other practices, such as *mariage coutumier,* in the process of making love grow.

38. In line with the sound pedagogical principles of a gradual and comprehensive personal growth, proximate preparation must not neglect formation for the social and ecclesial tasks proper to those who will have new families as a result of their marriage. Family intimacy should not be conceived as being closed in on itself, but rather as a capacity to interiorize the human and Christian riches inherent in married life in view of an ever greater giving to others. Therefore in an open concept of the family, married and family life requires the spouses to recognize themselves as subjects having rights but also duties towards society and the Church. In this regard, it will be very useful to encourage reading and reflecting on the following documents of the Church which are a rich and encouraging source of human and Christian wisdom: *Familiaris Consortio,* the Letter to Families *Gratissimam Sane,* the *Charter of the Rights of the Family, Evangelium Vitae,* and others.

39. The proximate preparation of young people should make them understand that the commitment they take on through the exchange of their consent "before the Church" makes it

necessary for them to begin a path of reciprocal fidelity in the engagement period. If necessary, any practices to the contrary must be abandoned. This human commitment will be enhanced by the specific gifts which the Holy Spirit gives to the engaged who invoke him.

40. Since Christian love is purified, perfected and elevated by Christ's love for the Church (cf. *GS* 49), the engaged should imitate this model and develop their awareness of self-giving which is always connected with the mutual respect and self-denial that help this love grow. Reciprocal self-giving thus implies more and more the exchange of spiritual gifts and moral support in order to make love and responsibility increase. "The indissolubility of marriage flows in the first place from the very essence of that gift: *the gift of one person to another person*. This reciprocal giving of self reveals the *spousal nature of love*" (*Gratissimam Sane,* 11).

41. Spousal spirituality, by involving human experience which is never separated from moral life, has its roots in Baptism and Confirmation. Preparation of the engaged should therefore include regaining the dynamism of the sacraments, with a special role of the sacraments of Reconciliation and the Eucharist. The sacrament of Reconciliation glorifies divine mercy toward human misery and makes the vitality of Baptism and the dynamism of Confirmation grow. From this the pedagogy of redeemed love is strengthened which lets the greatness of God's mercy be discovered before the drama of man, created by God and wonderfully redeemed. By celebrating the memory of Christ's giving to the Church, the Eucharist develops the affective love proper to marriage in daily giving to one's spouse and children, without forgetting

and overlooking that "the celebration which gives meaning to every other form of prayer and worship is found in *the family's actual daily life together*, if it is a life of love and self-giving" *(EV* 93).

42. For this kind of multi-faceted and harmonious preparation, the persons who will be in charge will have to be identified and given adequate formation. It would be useful to create a group, on different levels, of pastoral workers who are aware of being sent by the Church. This group should be composed of Christian married couples in particular, and include experts possibly in medicine, law, psychology, with a priest who will prepare them for the roles they will play.

43. The pastoral workers and persons in charge must have a solid doctrinal preparation and unquestionable fidelity to the Magisterium of the Church so that they will be able to transmit the truths of the faith and the responsibilities connected with marriage with sufficient in-depth knowledge and life witness. It is quite obvious that these pastoral workers, as educators, will also have to be capable of welcoming the engaged, whatever their social and culture extraction, intellectual formation and concrete capacities may be. Moreover, their faithful life witness and joyful giving are indispensable conditions for carrying out their task. Based on their own experiences in life and human problems, they can offer some starting-points for enlightening the engaged with Christian wisdom.

44. The above implies the need for an adequate formation programme for the pastoral workers. The formation leaders' preparation should prepare them to present the fundamental guidelines of marriage preparation which we have spoken

about with clear adherence to the Church's Magisterium, a suitable methodology and pastoral sensitivity, and also enable them to offer their specific contribution, according to their own expertise, to the immediate preparation (nos. 50-59). The pastoral workers ought to receive their formation in special Pastoral Institutes and be carefully chosen by the Bishop.

45. The final result of this period of proximate preparation should be a clear awareness of the essential characteristics of Christian marriage: unity, fidelity, indissolubility, fruitfulness; the conscience of faith regarding the priority of the sacramental Grace which associates the spouses, as subjects and ministers of the sacrament, to the love of Christ, the Bridegroom of the Church; the willingness to carry out the mission proper to families in the educational, social and ecclesial areas.

46. As *Familiaris Consortio* notes, the formative journey of young engaged persons should therefore include: deepening of personal faith and the rediscovery of the value of the sacraments and the experience of prayer. Specific preparation for life as a couple "will present marriage as an interpersonal relationship of a man and woman that has to be continually developed, and it will encourage those concerned to study the nature of conjugal sexuality and responsible parenthood, with the essential medical and biological knowledge connected with it. It will also acquaint those concerned with correct methods for the education of children, and will assist them in gaining the basic requisites for well-ordered family life" (*FC* 66); "preparation for the family apostolate, for fraternal solidarity and collaboration with other families, for active membership in groups, associations, movements and

undertakings set up for the human and Christian benefit of the family" (*Ibid.*).

Moreover, the engaged should be helped beforehand to learn how to preserve and cultivate married love later, interpersonal, marital communication, the virtues and difficulties of conjugal life, and how to overcome the inevitable conjugal "crises".

47. However, the centre of this preparation must be a reflection in the faith on the sacrament of Marriage through the Word of God and the guidance of the Magisterium. The engaged should be made aware that to become "una caro" (*Matthew* 19:6) in Christ, through the Spirit in Christian marriage, means imprinting a new form of baptismal life on their existence. Through the sacrament, their love will become a concrete expression of Christ's love for his Church (cf *LG* 11). In the light of the sacramentality, the married acts themselves, responsible procreation, educational activity, the communion of life, and the apostolic and missionary spirit connected with the life of Christian spouses are to be considered valid moments of Christian experience. Although still not in a sacramental way, Christ sustains and accompanies the journey of grace and growth of the engaged toward the participation in his mystery of union with the Church.

48. With regard to a possible Directory that will bring together the best experiences with marriage preparation, it seems useful to recall what the Holy Father John Paul II stated in his concluding Discourse to the General Assembly of the Pontifical Council for the Family held from September 30 - October 5, 1991: "It is essential that the time and care necessary should be devoted to *doctrinal* preparation. The

31

security of the content must be the centre and essential goal of the courses in a perspective which makes spouses more aware of the celebration of the Sacrament of Marriage and everything that flows from it regarding the responsibility of the family. Questions concerning the unity and indissolubility of marriage, and all that regards the meaning of the union and of procreation in married life and its specific act, must be treated faithfully and accurately, according to the clear teaching of the Encyclical *Humanae Vitae* (cf. nn. 11-12). This is equally true for everything that pertains to the gift of life which parents must accept responsibly and joyfully as the Lord's collaborators. The courses should not only emphasise what concerns the mature and vigilant freedom of those who want to contract marriage, but also their own mission as parents, the first educators of their children and their first evangelizers".

With deep satisfaction, this Pontifical Council observes that the tendency is growing towards greater commitment and awareness of the importance and dignity of the engagement period. Similarly, it urges that the specific courses will not be so brief as to reduce them to a mere formality. On the contrary, they should provide sufficient time for a good, clear presentation of the fundamental subjects indicated earlier.[3]

The course can be carried out in the individual parishes, if there are enough engaged persons and well-prepared collaborators, in the Episcopal or forane Vicariats, or in

---

[3] Pastoral care will suggest the ways and means for attaining the goal. For example, at least an entire week or four weekends, including Saturday and Sunday, would be necessary, or one afternoon monthly throughout the whole year.

parish co-ordinating structures. Sometimes they can be given by persons in charge of family movements, associations or apostolic groups guided by a competent priest. This is an area which should be co-ordinated by a *diocesan organism* that works on behalf of the Bishop. Without neglecting the various aspects of psychology, medicine and other human sciences, the content should be centred on the *natural and Christian doctrine of marriage*.

49. In proximate preparation, especially today, the engaged must be given formation and strengthened in the values concerning the defense of human life. Particularly in view of the fact that they will become the domestic church and "Sanctuary of life" (*EV* 92), they will become part in a new way of the "people of life and for life" (*EV* 6, 101). The contraceptive mentality which is prevalent today in so many places, and the widespread, permissive laws with all they imply in terms of contempt for life from the moment of conception to death, constitute a series of multiple attacks to which the family is exposed and wounded in the most intimate part of its mission, and which impede its development according to the requirements of authentic human growth (cf. *Centesimus Annus,* 39). Therefore, today more than before, formation is needed of the minds and hearts of the members of new families not to conform to the prevailing mentality. In this way, through their own new family life, one day they will be able to contribute towards creating and developing the culture of life by respecting and welcoming new lives in their love, as the testimony and expression of the proclamation, celebration and service to every life (cf. *EV* 83-84, 86, 93).

C. Immediate preparation

50. If a suitable itinerary and specific courses have been followed and have worked well during the period of proximate formation (cf. n. 32ss.), the aims of immediate preparation could consist of the following:

a) A synthesis of the previous preparation, especially its doctrinal, moral and spiritual content, thus filling in eventual gaps in basic formation;

b) Experiences of prayer (retreats, spiritual exercises for the engaged) in which the encounter with the Lord can make them discover the depth and beauty of the supernatural life;

c) A suitable liturgical preparation which also envisages the active participation of the engaged, with special attention to the Sacrament of Reconciliation;

d) Good use of the canonical talks that are envisaged with the parish priest, so that everyone can get to know one another better.

These ends will be achieved through special meetings of a more intensive nature.

51. The pastoral usefulness and positive experience of marriage preparation courses show that they can be dispensed with *only for proportionally serious reasons*. Therefore, if couples present themselves with the urgency of celebrating their marriage soon and without proximate preparation, the parish priest and his co-workers will have the responsibility of offering them some occasions to make up an adequate knowledge of the doctrinal, moral and sacramental aspects set out in the proximate preparation for marriage and finally include them in the phase of immediate preparation.

This is required because of the necessity to personalize

the formative itineraries in a real way, to take every occasion to deepen the meaning of what takes place in the sacrament, but without rejecting those who show they are well disposed towards the faith and the sacrament just because they were absent from some stages of preparation.

52. The immediate preparation for the sacrament of Marriage must find suitable occasions to introduce the engaged couple to the rite of marriage. As well as deepening the Christian doctrine on marriage and the family with particular attention to moral duties, in this preparation the engaged should be guided to take an informed and active part in the marriage celebration, and understand the meaning of the liturgical actions and texts.

53. This preparation for the sacrament of Marriage should be the culmination of a catechesis which helps engaged Christians to retrace their sacramental journey intelligently. It is important that they know that they are uniting themselves in marriage as persons baptized in Christ, and that they should behave in conformity to the Holy Spirit in their family life. Thus it is right that future spouses dispose themselves for the celebration of marriage so that it may be valid, worthy and fruitful, by receiving the sacrament of Penance (cf. *Catechism of the Catholic Church,* n. 1622). The liturgical preparation for the sacrament of Marriage should make the most of the elements of ritual that are currently available. To indicate a clearer relationship between the nuptial sacrament and the paschal mystery, the celebration of marriage is normally set within the celebration of the Eucharist.

54. In order to make the Church visible in the diocese and articulate this in the parishes, it is understandable that all the

canonical-pastoral preparation for marriage should culminate in the parish and diocese. Thus it is more in conformity with the ecclesial meaning of the sacrament for the marriage to be celebrated normally in the church of the parish community to which the spouses belong (*CIC*, Canon 1115).

It is desirable that the whole parish community take part in this celebration, around the families and friends of the engaged. Provisions for this should be made in various dioceses, taking local situations into account, but also decisively favouring truly ecclesial pastoral action.

55. Those who will take an active part in the liturgy should be invited also to prepare themselves properly for the sacrament of Reconciliation and the Eucharist. It should be explained to the witnesses that they are not only the guarantors of a juridical act, but also representatives of the Christian community which, through them, participates in a sacramental act relevant to it, because a new family is a cell of the Church. On account of its essentially social character, marriage calls for the participation of society and this is to be expressed through the presence of the witnesses.

56. The family is the most appropriate place where, according to the decision of the local Ordinary and through the common priesthood, parents can carry out sacred acts and administer some sacramentals, such as for example in the context of Christian Initiation, in the joyful or sad events of daily life, in saying grace at meals. A special place should be given to family prayer. This creates an atmosphere of faith within the home and will be the means of living out a richer fatherhood and motherhood for the children, teaching them to pray and introducing them to the gradual discovery of the mystery of God and personal dialogue with him. Parents

should remember that they carry out their mission of proclaiming the Gospel of life through educating their children (c.f. *Evangelium vitae,* 92).

57. Immediate preparation is a propitious occasion to begin the ongoing pastoral care of marriage and the family. From this point of view, the preparation needs to be carried out so that spouses know their mission in the Church. Here they can be helped by the richness offered by specific family movements, so as to cultivate a spirituality of marriage and the family and the way they fulfil their tasks within the family, the Church and society.

58. The preparation of the engaged should be accompanied by sincere and deep devotion to Mary, Mother of the Church, the *Queen of the Family.* The engaged themselves should be taught to recognize that Mary's presence is as active in the family, the Domestic Church, as it is in the wider Church. Likewise they should be taught to imitate Mary in her virtues. Thus the Holy Family, the home of Jesus, Mary and Joseph, makes the engaged discover "how sweet and irreplaceable education in the family is" (Paul VI, *Discourse at Nazareth,* January 5, 1964).

59. A gift and enrichment for the whole Church will be sharing with others whatever is creatively proposed in various communities to make these proximate and immediate phases of preparation deeper and more adequate.

III

THE CELEBRATION OF MARRIAGE

60. Preparation for marriage leads to married life, through the celebration of the sacrament, which is the culmination of the journey of preparation which the spouses have made and the source and origin of their married life. Therefore, the celebration cannot be reduced only to a ceremony, the product of culture and sociological conditioning. Nevertheless, praiseworthy customs that belong to various peoples or ethnic groups can be brought into the celebration (cf. *Sacrosanctum Concilium, 77; Familiaris Consortio, 67*), provided that they express above all the coming together of the ecclesial assembly as a sign of the faith of the Church, which recognizes in the sacrament the presence of the Risen Lord uniting the spouses to the Love of the Trinity.

61. Through diocesan liturgical commissions, the bishops should give precise directions and supervise how these are applied in practice, in order to put into effect, in the celebration of marriage, what is indicated in article 32 of the Constitution on the Liturgy, so that even externally the equality of the faithful may be evident and, further, that any appearance of pomp be avoided. The active participation of those present is to be favoured in every way. Suitable materials should be provided to help them comprehend and savour the richness of the rite.

62. Mindful that where two or three are gathered in the name of Christ (cf. *Matthew* 18:20), there he is present, a

restrained style of celebration (which should also continue in the feasting that follows) must not only be an expression of the community of faith, but a motive for praising the Lord. To celebrate getting married in the Lord and before the Church means professing that the gift of grace made to the spouses by the presence and love of Christ and His Spirit calls for a practical response, with a life of worship in spirit and truth, in the Christian family, the "domestic church". Precisely because the celebration is to be understood not only as a legal act but also as a moment in the history of salvation of those being married, and through their common priesthood, for the good or the Church and society, it will be good to help all present to take part actively in the celebration itself.

63. It will be the duty of whoever presides to make use of the possibilities which the ritual itself offers, especially in its second typical edition promulgated in 1991 by the Congregation for Divine Worship and the Discipline of the Sacraments, so as to highlight the role of the ministers of the sacrament who, for Christians of the Latin Rite, are the spouses themselves, as well as the sacramental value of the community celebration. With the formula of the exchange of consent, the spouses will always remember the personal, ecclesial and social aspect gained from this consent for all their life, as a gift of one to the other even unto death.[4]

---

[4] The Congregation for the Doctrine of the Faith teaches that marriage between Christians cannot be treated as something private and recalls the doctrine and discipline of the Church: "In fidelity to the words of Jesus Christ, the Church affirms that a new union cannot be recognized as valid if the preceding marriage was valid. If the divorced are remarried civilly, they find themselves in a situation that objectively contravenes

The Eastern Rite reserves the role of the minister of marriage to the assisting priest. In any case, according to the law of the Church, the presence of a priest or a duly authorized minister is necessary for the validity of the matrimonial union and clearly sets forth the public and social meaning of the spousal covenant, both for the Church and for all of society.

64. Bearing in mind that marriage is normally celebrated during Mass (cf. *Sacrosanctum Concilium*, 78; *Familiaris Consortio*, 57), when dealing with a marriage between a Catholic and a baptized non-Catholic, the celebration will take place according to the special liturgical and canonical provisions (cf. *Ordo Celebrandi Matrimonium* - OCM, 79-117).

65. The celebration will lead to more active participation if apposite introductions to the meaning of the liturgical texts and the content of the prayers are used. The simplicity of these introductions should favour recollection and understanding the importance of the celebration (cf. *OCM*, 52, 59, 87, 93, 99), and avoid turning the celebration into a didactic moment.

66. The celebrant who presides[5] and presents the ecclesial

God's law. Consequently, they cannot receive Holy Communion as long as this situation persists." (Congregation for the Doctrine of the Faith, *Letter to the Bishops of the Catholic Church concerning the Reception of Holy Communion by Divorced and Remarried Members of the Faithful*, n. 4, September 14, 1994).

[5] Cf. *OCM*, 24; *CIC*, Canon 1111; cf. *OCM*, 25 and 118-151; *CIC*, Canon 1112.2; 1108.2.

meaning of the marriage commitment for the assembly, will try to involve those who are being married, together with their relatives and the witnesses, so that they can comprehend the structure of the rite. This applies especially to the most characteristic parts, such as: the Word of God, the consent exchanged and ratified, the blessing of the signs that symbolize marriage (rings etc.), the solemn blessing of the spouses, the reference to the spouses in the heart of the Eucharistic Prayer. "The various liturgies abound in prayers of blessing and epiclesis asking God's grace and blessing on the new couple, especially the bride." (*Catechism of the Catholic Church,* n. 1624). It will also be necessary to explain the gesture of imposing hands on the "subject ministers" of the sacrament. Standing, the sign of peace or other rites determined by the competent authorities, etc. will be appropriately brought to the attention of all present.

67. To achieve a style of celebration at once restrained and noble, whoever presides should be helped by the presence of assistant ministers, of people who will animate and sustain the singing of the faithful, lead the responses and proclaim the Word of God. With particular concrete attention to those who are being married and their situation, and absolutely avoiding any preference for persons, the celebrant should adapt himself to the truth of the signs used in the liturgical action. Thus, in welcoming and greeting those about to be married, their parents if present, the witnesses and others who attend, he will be the living spokesman of the community that welcomes those who are being married.

68. The proclamation of the Word of God is to be made by suitable and prepared lectors. Thy can be chosen from among those present, especially witnesses, family members, friends,

41

but it does not seem appropriate for the bride and groom to be lectors. In fact, they are the primary receivers of the proclaimed Word of God. However, the choice of readings can be made in accord with the engaged couple during the phase of immediate preparation. In this way they will more easily bear the Word of God in mind so as to put it into practice.

69. The homily, which is obligatory, will have as its centre the presentation of the "great mystery" being celebrated before God, the Church and society. "Saint Paul uses a concise phrase in reference to family life: it is a *great mystery* (*Ephesians* 5: 32)". (*Gratissimam Sane,* 19). Beginning with the proclaimed texts of the Word of God and/or the liturgical prayers, light should focus on the sacrament, hence the consequences for the life of the spouses and their families should be illustrated. Superfluous personal references to the spouses should be avoided.

70. If the rite takes place during the celebration of Mass, the gifts may be brought to the altar by the spouses themselves. In any case, the well-prepared prayer of the faithful should be neither too long nor lacking in concrete content. As may be pastorally appropriate, Holy Communion can be given under both Species.

71. Care should be taken that the details of the marriage celebration are characterized by a restrained, simple and authentic style. The festive tone should not be disturbed by excessive display.

72. The solemn blessing of the spouses recalls that the gift of the Holy Spirit is invoked in the sacrament of Marriage. Through this gift, the married couple are made more constant in their mutual concord and spiritually sustained in carrying

out their mission, also in the difficulties of their future life. In the framework of this celebration, it will certainly be appropriate to present the Holy Family of Nazareth as a model of life for Christian spouses.

73. With regard to the periods of remote, proximate and immediate preparation, while it is good to bring together actual experiences in order to effect a major change of mentality and practices associated with the celebration, pastoral workers should take care to follow and make comprehensible what is already set down and established by the liturgical rite. It is obvious that such understanding will depend on the whole process of preparation and the community's level of Christian maturity.

*   *   *

Anyone can take note that some elements are proposed here for an organic preparation of the faithful called to the sacrament of Marriage. Especially in the first five years of married life, it would be desirable to follow up the young couples through post-marriage courses, to be carried out in parishes or deaneries, according to the norm of the Directory for the Pastoral Care of the Family, mentioned earlier in nos. 14 and 15, in connection with the Apostolic Exhortation, *Familiaris Consortio,* 66.

The Pontifical Council for the Family *entrusts to the Episcopal Conferences* these guidelines for their own directories.

The pastoral concern of the Episcopal Conferences and individual Bishops will ensure that these guidelines are put into action in the ecclesial communities. Thus each of the faithful will understand better that the sacrament of Marriage, *a great mystery* (*Ephesians* 5: 21ss) is a vocation for so many in the People of God.

Vatican City State, May 13, 1996

ALFONSO Cardinal LÓPEZ TRUJILLO
*President of the Pontifical Council
for the Family*

✠ Most Rev. FRANCISCO GIL HELLÍN
Secretary